Josh Allen: The Inspiring Story of One of Football's Star Quarterbacks

An Unauthorized Biography

By: Clayton Geoffreys

Visit my website at www.claytongeoffreys.com
Cover photo by All-Pro Reels is licensed under CC BY-SA 2.0 / modified from original

Table of Contents

Foreword

Being able to call yourself the highest-drafted professional football player from Wyoming is already an accomplishment. And that was just the start of Josh Allen's NFL career. Since then, he has quickly emerged as a steadfast leader and future star quarterback in the league. While he began as a backup quarterback to Nathan Peterman, Josh Allen quickly became the starting quarterback to the Buffalo Bills and helped guide the team to a 10-win season and their second playoff appearance since 1999. He'd follow that season with another breakout year, as he'd set multiple Bills' records while also being selected to the Pro Bowl. Josh Allen has come a long way, and he still has a lot more football ahead of him. Thank you for purchasing *Josh Allen: The Inspiring Story of One of Football's Star Quarterbacks*. In this unauthorized biography, we will learn Josh Allen's incredible life story and impact on the game of football. Hope you enjoy and if you do, please do not forget to leave a review!

Also, check out my website at claytongeoffreys.com to join my exclusive list where I let you know about my latest books. To thank you for your purchase, you can go to my site to download a free copy of *33 Life Lessons: Success Principles, Career Advice & Habits of Successful People*. In the book, you'll learn from some of the greatest thought leaders of different industries on what it takes to become successful and how to live a great life.

Cheers,

Clayton Geoffreys

Visit me at www.claytongeoffreys.com

Introduction

"He's everything you want in a quarterback. He's a true leader." [i]

– Stefon Diggs

Cinderella stories among quarterbacks in the NFL are very few and far between. Most every star passer in the game has come from a distinguished background. Even if they did not grow up in a great childhood, they were high school and college stars with high aspirations and illustrious promise.

The story of Josh Allen, however, is unique. He grew up on a farm in the middle of nowhere in California, and the nearest town was some thirty minutes away. He showed promise as a passer in high school, but hardly anyone wanted him. He had to play for a community college first before the University of Wyoming gave him a call and asked him to come aboard.

Even then, the chances of Allen getting to the pro level were nearly remote. Only three other quarterbacks in the game's history were drafted out of Wyoming, and none of them were picked in the first five rounds, and only one came after 1960.

But Josh Allen wanted to defy the odds and do something that no said believed he could do. He went to Wyoming and stunned scouts, throwing for just under 5,000 yards and 44 touchdowns in two seasons. He set many single-season records at the school, but people still doubted him because of where he came from. [iii]

He gained the reputation of a mobile gun-slinger with a big arm and exquisite leadership qualities, but NFL teams still doubted him because of his background. With his kind of talent, he would typically be a surefire top-five pick in the NFL Draft, but rumors swirled about his lack of playing big-time competition and tendencies to be inaccurate.

While no one can blame the Cleveland Browns for selecting Baker Mayfield with the first-round pick, other teams followed by passing on Allen. The New York Jets decided to pick Sam Darnold over Allen, a move that they must undoubtedly regret today. The Broncos could have used a quarterback but selected Bradley Chubb instead, putting their faith behind Case Keenum, who is no longer with the team.

After the Colts selected guard Quentin Nelson with the sixth pick, the Buffalo Bills were in a prime position to get the quarterback they wanted. Josh Allen had always been the guy on the top of their draft board, and when he fell to them with the seventh overall pick, they took no time turning their card in.

Before Allen, the Bills had a shaky quarterback history between the era of Jim Kelly and Allen. Since Kelly retired, Buffalo struggled to find a franchise quarterback and missed the playoffs nearly every year. From 2000 to 2017, the Bills had just two winning seasons and zero ten-win seasons. They had just one postseason appearance.

Since Allen arrived and took over the starting position in 2018, the Bills have compiled two postseason appearances, one being an AFC Championship appearance, and ended the New England Patriots of 11 straight AFC East crowns.

More impressively, Allen has helped guide the Bills to a 23-9 record over the past two seasons. The last time Buffalo won 23 games in two seasons was 1992-1993.

Allen has proven to NFL scouts who doubted his accuracy and ability to turn Buffalo back around into winners that they were wrong about him. Despite a subpar rookie season, Allen has made incredible progression. In 2018, he threw ten touchdowns and 12 picks and finished with a 67.4 rating. In 2019, he threw 20 touchdowns and nine picks, finishing with an 85.3 rating. And in 2020, Allen threw 37 touchdowns compared to just ten interceptions and an incredible 107.2 rating.[ii]

Only Aaron Rodgers finished above Josh Allen for the 2020 Most Valuable Player. Allen finished in the top five in almost every single quarterback statistical category in 2020. This comes after finishing nearly at the bottom in almost every statistical category in 2018.[ii]

But Allen's success goes beyond just his ability to throw a football. He has built trust in his players, particularly Stefon Diggs, the team's number one wide receiver, who was traded to Buffalo in 2020 and found a new home that he is happy at because of Allen. Diggs has said that one of the things that separate Allen from other leaders is that he puts trust in you and instills confidence in your mind.

"He's one of a kind," Diggs said. "He's a true leader."[i]

Diggs said he would not be as successful as he has been in Buffalo without Allen. He cares about his players and connects with them. Allen reached out to him when Diggs was traded to Buffalo despite being quarantined because of the COVID-19 virus. The two put on headsets from their separate homes and played Call of Duty together and got to know each other better from the very start. The relationship built into a "bromance" that even Stefon Diggs' brother said was one of a kind.

The 2020 season did not end the way the Bills had hoped despite making incredible progress. It ended at Arrowhead Field in Kansas City in a lopsided loss in the AFC Championship to the defending Super Bowl champions at the time. Most would call it part of the process. You can't go from Earth to Mars in one day. It takes time. Since 2018, the Bills have been moving steadily forward, and now comes the 2021 season alongside the Chiefs as the favorites to try and win the Super Bowl away from Tom Brady and the Buccaneers.

"I think he (Allen) answered quite a few of the questions that were out there about him maybe from outside this building, specifically about his play. And I know that the comforting piece to me about Josh is he's going to go back to work," Bills coach Sean McDermott said. "He's an extremely driven young man with a bright future and he's done a great job leading our team this season in particular." [iv]

Allen's story is truly one of an underdog excelling to become a superstar. He grew up in a town with only around 7,000 people and was very rarely heard by anyone coming out of high school. But he proved that no matter where you come from, you can make it to the big time.

He's a big kid with an even bigger heart, evidenced by his contributions to John R. Oishei Children's Hospital in Buffalo. Allen spends a lot of time at the hospital working with kids and helping to lift their spirits.

When Josh Allen's grandmother passed away in December 2020, the community, nicknamed Bills Mafia, rallied around their star quarterback and donated more than $1 million to the Patricia Allen Fund at Oishei hospital.

"At a loss for words, Buffalo," Allen responded in a tweet. "I love you." [vi]

Buffalo is the perfect place for Josh because there is a mutual connection between the two. Not only has Josh fallen in love with the fans there and admires them, but the fans love him. They have rallied around him and taken him into their homes.

It's hard to find a city that respects a leader like they do Josh Allen. He has helped to bring not just football back to Buffalo but helped inspire the younger generation. Seeing how he carries himself on and off the field is a blessing in today's day and age. He is the perfect role model for the youth of America. He has a winning and positive attitude, believes in teamwork, leads by example, and helps those who need it most.

A couple of days after his grandmother's passing, Allen released another statement about all of the donations and his feeling towards the fans in Buffalo. "I can't tell you how special it is to see the outpouring of support for me and my family during this tough time," Allen said. "The donations made to OCH in honor of my grandmother would make her so proud. Thank you Bills Mafia! It is an honor to be your quarterback." [vi]

Buffalo is lucky to have Josh Allen, and young athletes everywhere are fortunate to have a role model like him to emulate and look up to.

Chapter 1: Early Life and Childhood

"I had, in my opinion, the greatest role model in the world in my dad." [v]

- Josh Allen

Joshua Patrick Allen was born on May 21, 1996, in the small town of Firebaugh, California, to Joel and Lavonne Allen. Josh has a brother, Jason, and two sisters, Nicala and Makenna.

Josh grew up on a farm in Firebaugh and helped his dad when he could. His dad worked incredibly hard on the 2,000-acre farm, producing cotton, cantaloupe, wheat, and other products to bring in money and keep the family happy. The farm was started by grandfather, Buzz, who died in 1975 and handed it over to his son.

Buzz was a legend in Firebaugh, having emigrated from Sweden and settling in the small town. He was so revered there that they named the Firebaugh High

School football field after him when he donated land to the school.

Josh loved his dad a lot and respected the heck out of him for how hard of a worker he was. His dad was his role model growing up and taught him the importance of doing whatever it takes to excel and respecting others. But there was no way he wanted to grow up doing what his father was doing. He did not want to join the family business. He wanted to be an athlete.

"I had, in my opinion, the greatest role model in the world in my dad," Josh said. "The things he did for our family to keep food on the table, he's a smart businessman and a hard worker. It's something that I look up to, how hard he works to support our family. Having to see your dad wake up before sunrise, coming home after sunset, and helping him in the 105, 110-degree weather … there's no days off. It's something that's special to me, something that I believe has helped me get to where I am today." [v]

Joel's life was the farm and managing it to perfection. He had a tough job and was devoted to it.

"I make sure everybody else does their job," Joel said. "And I'm kind of the bookkeeper slash accountant. All the employee-related matters, labor issues. You name it; I do it." [ix]

Josh chipped in and helped as much he could. He helped a lot with irrigation. "Going down every single row with a little hoe," the Mountain West preseason offensive player of the year said. "Literally, every single row. It took a long time, and it was 100 degrees out there. You definitely got either burnt or a really good tan." [ix]

According to Joel, working on the farm taught his kids responsibility and hard work. It taught him that nothing will ever be handed to you and that you must go out there and earn everything in life.

Joel inspired Josh a lot, and Josh admitted that he would not be where he is today without his father.

Every time Josh is pushed to the limit and thinks he can't go anymore, he thinks of his dad and the hard work and sacrifices he made for his family, and it pushes Josh to go that extra mile.

Josh's efforts on the farm got him honors from the FFA, also known as the Future Farmers of America. He was awarded San Joaquin Regional Proficiency and National Proficiency Silver Honors in Grain Production Entrepreneurship. His teacher helped him by writing a national letter that showcased all that he accomplished, not just in sports but also his honors and hard work in farming. [ix]

Josh would help his dad out on the farm from time to time, but he tried to avoid it as much as possible by being active. He wanted to be an athlete when he grew up, not a farmer. He loved competition. He stayed busy playing multiple sports growing up, including football, basketball, baseball, and soccer. He even did more minor sports such as karate, gymnastics, and swimming. Anything to keep him active, he would do.

"Growing up, my dad was very adamant on me doing sports, and I don't think he would want me to go in the farming business because of some of the hardships that he's had to endure," Josh said. "... He's very tactical in his approach to farming, and it's something that you can't just take over and run with. It's a life of learning." [ix]

The hardships on the farm got harder as Josh got into high school and college. Firebaugh experienced a massive drought that impacted the farm. It motivated Josh to be successful when he got older to give money to help out his dad's farm battling the growing drought problem. It was not far away from Firebaugh, where wildfires ravaged towns due to a lack of rain. However, since then, things have improved. Josh has given back financially, and the area has received a lot more rain, so it could resume growing good cotton.

Part of the reason why Josh loved sports was that his whole family was competitive. His two sisters and brothers always played sports and competed against each other for fun around the farm. But when it came to football, Josh was the best. The family built sports areas around their farm, including a green pitch, a volleyball court, and a mini football field.

"For as long as I can remember, sitting there in our living room watching *Monday Night Football*, running around the living room table," Josh said when asked when his interest in football first brewed. "Me and my brother made tracks around that. We'd run around it, and my dad would throw us the ball while he was watching the game. There were a few dents in the walls, some broken vases, stuff like that." [v]

Josh played youth football in Firebaugh, which was huge in town given how small the population was. Josh developed as one of the best players on his team and became quarterback in the youth league.

The kids that Josh played against in the youth league were those that he'd play with in high school. After all, there were no high schools in town besides Firebaugh High School unless you wanted to travel a half-hour and attend a school in Fresno. The town and all of the boys were tight-knit.

Allen loved watching sports growing up, not just football. He enjoyed going to see the San Francisco Giants play baseball and meet the players after the game. While positive interactions with superstars inspire most athletes, it was a negative interaction that motivated Josh to become a better person when he grew up.

After one of the Giants games, Josh and his family waited to meet some of the Giants players and get an autograph. Josh had always been a huge fan of Barry Bonds despite the allegations against him for steroid use. Josh desperately wanted to meet him and get his autograph. It would make his day.

But after that night, Josh Allen would never root for Barry Bonds again.

"We were in the tunnel and Bonds had a really good game," Josh said. "It was probably an hour after the game, and there were maybe ten kids out waiting. My parents were begging us, like, 'Let's go, let's go. He's not coming out.' I told them, 'Yeah, he is. He'll sign our autographs.' Sure enough, he came out, and like I said, there are probably ten kids left. Instead of looking and waving and maybe even giving us fist bumps or whatever, he just kind of turned his cap to the side and kept walking. That just left an impression on me, like, I don't want to root for this guy anymore. It bothered me so much." [vii]

It hurt Josh. He always looked up to Bonds, and it left a negative impact on him like he did not care. Josh made a vow to his parents that he would never allow himself to be like Barry Bonds. That he will always acknowledge children and fans, even if he had a bad game. These fans come to see you, and you need to at least appreciate and acknowledge them.

So far in his career, Allen has lived up to his promise. Every time at training camp, you see Josh go over to the kids and give them high-fives or fist bumps. He visits hospitals regularly and tries to lift spirits when they're down. After games, he spends time signing autographs and showing fans respect and courtesy for coming to see them.

That's who Josh Allen is. He is one of the kindest and most respectable athletes today. Some of it is because of that moment with Barry Bonds, but also because of his family and how his parents raised him.

"I just want to try and be a good person off the field," Josh said. "Without being able to go in person and doing some of these benefits and some of these foundation events, it's a little tougher, obviously. I wish things were back to normal where we could go and do these things. I think something as simple as me showing up somewhere or saying hello to a kid, that can really impact somebody or some organization in a major way." [vii]

It was always a lesson that Josh lived by. He always remembered that moment as a kid, and when he is out with kids now, he puts himself in their shoes and thinks of how they want to be treated. He knows that they want a smile, and the fact that Josh is successful today, just visiting a sick patient and putting a smile on their face can go a long way to lifting their spirits.

Josh's heart was big from the very beginning. In school, he was always one of the most humble and gracious kids around. He liked to volunteer his time around town, although the town was so small.

Josh spent a lot of time helping his dad and playing sports, but he also made time for his mom. She ran The Farmer's Daughter Restaurant and recruited her sons and daughters to help her out when they could. During lunchtime, Josh and his brother would stop by the restaurant and help their mom out with washing dishes and helping out when they were short-staffed. He didn't get any pay for it, but he did get free lunch.

"I'd come back, I'd have a payroll, I'd be back there (working)," Lavonne Allen said. "I was constantly on my phone because there's ordering of the supplies and a lot of stuff that has to go on, that has to be taken of, whether you're there or not. And for 13 weeks, we traveled. Come Christmas time, I was an exhausted mess." [viii]

That was the Allen family in a nutshell. They were always busy from the top down to the bottom. Whether it was work, school, or sports, there was not much time to relax.

As Josh prepared for high school, he had to decide between attending Firebaugh or Dos Palos High School, which was 15 miles up the road. But Firebaugh High School meant a lot to Josh. That is where his grandfather donated land, and he felt that there was a piece of family history there. Even the gymnasium was named after his grandfather, Buzz.

Chapter 2: High School Career

"Yeah, they blew it." [x]

- Bill Magnusson, Firebaugh High School coach on Fresno State passing on Allen

Josh Allen did not enter high school as a huge prospect that everyone in the area thought was going to be the next Derek Carr, another famous California quarterback who went to college 40 miles from Firebaugh at Fresno State. He started his first couple of years developing on junior varsity. He didn't even play on the varsity team until his junior year.

Allen's size was adequate but not a huge factor. He was barely 6 feet tall when he entered high school. By the time he was a senior, he was 6'2" and 180 pounds. Today, as a player for the Buffalo Bills, he's 6'5" and 237. He just kept growing.

As a sophomore on the JV team, Allen played in seven games. He put up impressive numbers, throwing 103 completions on 173 attempts for 1,645 yards and 21 touchdowns. He also ran for 221 yards and two scores. His performance on the junior varsity team helped pave the way for him to play varsity and impressed Bill Magnusson, the Firebaugh High School head coach. [xi]

Allen was not a one-sport guy, though. As he got older, he also loved baseball and would play for the Firebaugh baseball team in his final three seasons, starting on junior varsity. Allen put up solid numbers on the diamond, hitting .409 his sophomore season. In his three years in baseball, he averaged .352 and drove in 75 runs. He totaled 16 doubles and eight triples. [xi]

Allen also was a part-time pitcher, appearing 21 times over three seasons and posting a 7-2 record. Given his strong arm in football, it was apparent that he was challenging to hit in baseball. But he did not like pitching a lot for fear that it could affect his arm in football, which was a sport that he loved just a bit more than baseball.

Josh spent many offseasons playing baseball and basketball or helping his dad on the farm. These things tampered with Josh's development in football to a degree. But before his junior season, Josh worked harder than ever before and told his football coach that things would change with him as the team's leader.

One of those things was winning more games and beating rival Mendota High School. Mendota had been a thorn in Firebaugh's side for so long in youth leagues and high school, and they had given Magnusson headaches.

"I think in one year in Pop Warner, they beat us like 58-0," said Bill Magnusson, then Firebaugh's head football coach. "... Not only Josh, a lot of kids on that team had told me that they weren't even going to play football in high school because they were so bad." [ix]

According to Magnusson, before Allen taking over the reins his junior season, they had been outscored 242-18 by Mendota over the last four seasons. But Josh said that was going to change.

"Josh's goal was, 'I want me and my brothers to work hard to beat Mendota,'" Magnusson said. "'That's our rival.'" ix

Allen was not afraid of anything. Growing up, he had already been through adversity, helping his father and watching him fight like no one else has fought before to keep the farm alive.

Allen helped make Firebaugh's football team better in a year that they were not supposed to be good. Firebaugh had many seniors and was picked by some to finish last or second to last in their conference. Tougher yet, Mendota was ranked number one in the valley by the time they played Firebaugh.

But Firebaugh and Josh Allen exceeded expectations. That junior season, Allen threw for 275 yards and three touchdowns against Mendota, and the Firebaugh Eagles finally beat them 25-20 in the second-to-last game of the year. [ix]

That junior season, Allen started 11 games and had eight multi-touchdown games. Two games that season, he threw four touchdowns. He finished a completion percentage of just over 50 percent and 2,208 yards. He threw 26 touchdowns as opposed to ten interceptions. He also rushed for 201 yards. As a starter, Allen went 7-4, much better than anyone thought they would finish. [ix]

Coaches said one of the most respectable things about Josh was how he carried himself and acted around others. He was mature and respectful. There were moments that he got upset when the team did not make plays, and he needed coaches to step in and remind him that things would be okay.

"There were some times when he was younger, in his junior year (at Firebaugh), when I had to get a little tough on him," offensive coordinator Mike Martinez said. I told him, 'Josh, you're not going to always be perfect. I'm telling you. These kids are not out here to drop it. They're here to catch it. This O-line's here to protect you, not to let them come in and tackle you.' And he got it. That's what I love about Josh, because every time I talked to him, he was able to take it in and handle it the right way. Never disrespectful." [ix]

As he entered his senior season, Allen hoped to get some college teams to visit and show some interest. But he wasn't getting any, and he realized that the only way to get their attention was to work harder and keep having great games, and also, to win.

"I just knew every time we put Josh out there, there was a good chance we were going to get a W," Magnusson said. [ix]

Magnusson was so impressed with Allen's arm, which was one of the strongest he had ever seen. He had NFL potential in him down the road with the way he composed himself as a quarterback and threw the ball.

"We'd do NFL catches where you've got to put two feet in," Magnusson said. "So (Allen) would do the catch. Coach Alex would throw the ball to him to demonstrate this is what I want, and Josh would drag a foot or drag two feet, and he'd make the catch, then he'd run 15 yards, turn around and throw the ball on a dime to the next kid who was running the out route. That kid would drag his foot, and the ball would be right on." [ix]

Firebaugh changed their offense because of Allen, catering to his strengths. Allen thrived in more of a spread offense. He had the speed to make plays with his legs if he had to and could throw on the run. His quick decision-making and vision were perfect for the offense that Magnusson and offensive coordinator Mike Martinez wanted to run.

"When Josh came along, I realized what the kid's ability was," Martinez said, "and he was able to open up our spread game, and obviously we were able to introduce the spread game as well." [ix]

That happened a lot in Josh's senior season. The Eagles started 9-0 before they faced their rival, Mendota. In those nine wins, Allen threw 28 touchdowns. He threw three or four touchdowns in all but one of his first nine games. [x]

Unfortunately, the 10th game was against Mendota, and the Eagles could not stun their rivals again. They lost 43-12 in what Magnusson would call Mendota's best-ever season. [x]

The Eagles won the next week over Immanuel in a game where Allen threw a career-high five touchdown passes and 442 yards. The victory in the first round of the playoffs advanced the Eagles to Division V Semifinals. Unfortunately, that game was against Mendota, a rematch from a couple of weeks back.

Again, Mendota dominated the Eagles in Allen's worst game of the year. The Eagles season ended 45-0 on the losing end. [x]

Allen was still a part of history. The school won a record ten games that season. Allen set a Firebaugh High School record with 33 touchdown passes, and he threw for 3,061 yards and had a .574 completion percentage. [x]

For Allen, he hoped that his football career was not over. He desperately wanted to play college football for someone. Unfortunately, no one came to visit. Part of that was because of where Firebaugh was located. It was in the middle of nowhere. It didn't get the recognition of other huge high schools in California.

The one school that Josh wanted to go to more than anything was Fresno State. It was his dream as a child to play there one day. He idolized Derek Carr, who played there when Josh was entering high school and was now a part of the Raiders. Josh had a picture taken with Derek Carr that he had framed and hanging in his room.

"From 8 or 9 years old, you knew he wanted to go to Fresno State," Allen's Pop Warner coach Chauncey Lee said. "This kid was *dying* to play there. The parents probably would have paid his tuition. He didn't even need a scholarship." [xi]

But Fresno State never called. Neither did any of the hundred or so schools that Josh, his family, and coaches sent emails to, trying to get them to come out and show interest in him.

Fresno State's head coach was Tim DeRuyter. The team had studied Allen, but when asked why they didn't pursue him, the answer was that Allen did not face stiff high school competition and would not be able to hold up at the Division I level. Fresno was concerned about his 180-pound frame. [v]

Other schools did not know much about him because Josh never attended any camps. Josh spent his offseason playing other sports and helping his family out, and to this day, he would tell you that he doesn't regret that. But the lack of exposure to colleges hurt his chances of getting a Division I scholarship.

Only one school talked to Josh Allen about playing football for them: Wyoming. But after showing interest, they then bailed out and didn't offer a scholarship. According to Magnusson, this was the best thing that happened to Allen because it lit a fire in him in future play.

"Some people think because you have an easier path, you must've been better than everybody else," Magnusson said. "The people I've known that are the greatest are the ones that have had the hardest path. He's had an uphill climb, but that's made him better." xi

Magnusson said to use the snubs by colleges as anger, to go out there and prove other people wrong and work as hard as you possibly could and show that you were worth the investment. There were avenues to take if you don't get a scholarship, and Allen would start to explore those. One of those was playing for a community college.

Allen enrolled at Reedley Community College, about 75 miles from Firebaugh High School. He planned on trying out for the football team there to get more views from schools and hopefully transfer to a Division I school. The chances of success were slim. After all, you never hear about successful quarterbacks who began their career at a community college. Allen would have to work harder than anyone to make it to the college and pro levels.

Chapter 3: College Career

Reedley Junior College

Josh Allen had some connections with Reedley College. Aaron Wilkins, Reedley's safeties coach, was married to Josh's cousin. He spread the word over to offensive coordinator Ernie Rodriguez to keep an eye on this kid in high school. Rodriguez loved what he saw, but Wilkins told him that the opportunity to recruit and land Allen at Reedley might never arise because another university may snag him.

Wilkins raved about Allen and how great of a kid he was personally. He was a leader and hard worker who would go to war with you, but also a kid who was easy to teach and was mature for his age. Rodriguez decided to travel to Firebaugh with Wilkins to watch Allen.

"It was a family affair, and that really sold me on him," said Rodriguez, who is now at College of the Sequoias. "I knew that he was a kid I wanted to bring in. I didn't recruit any other quarterbacks. He was the only one. I threw all my chips in on this kid." [xiii]

Rodriguez pushed hard to get Allen, despite the chances of losing him to a university. He put all of his chips on one guy. "I didn't recruit any other quarterbacks," Rodriguez said. "He was the only one I wanted. It was a full-court press to try and get him." [xiii]

Rodriguez lucked out. When Fresno turned Allen down and Wyoming rescinded their interest, Allen was open to going to Reedley and playing a year or two at the junior college to get interest from colleges.

Allen's decision to play at Reedley kept him in playing shape. He went there and spent the preseason learning, and by the team's second game, he was put in the game. Unfortunately, his first pass landed in an interception. It was not exactly the start he envisioned for his college career. He went 2-for-7 in that first game for 26 yards. [xiv]

He got some more playing time in his third game, but he only went 1-for-6 for 30 yards. But then, in the fourth game, Allen's career seemingly changed forever. Despite struggling badly in his first few games, coaches decided to let Allen use the read-option more in his play-calling, and he delivered.

Allen finally started some rhythm against Gavilan, tossing his first touchdown pass. He threw for 108 yards despite going just 5-for-16. But his ability to run the spread gave the offense a bounce. Allen kept it 21 times for 161 yards, rushing for four touchdowns in helping Reedley win 44-33. [xiv]

After that performance, the offense was Allen's. He would start the rest of the season and deliver great performances.

Against Fresno City on the road, he threw three touchdowns. The following week, he threw five. Against Cabrillo, he threw four. Then came the game that got the Wyoming Cowboys interested. Against

Merced College, Allen completed 28 passes for a school record 470 yards and seven touchdowns. He also ran for 46 yards, meaning that he had over 500 all-purpose yards. [xiv]

"After that game, even the people at Merced in the crowd were like, 'This guy's the real deal,'" Rodriguez. "And I said, 'Yup, he sure is.' That was the game where I said, 'Holy hell, if this guy keeps it up, this guy has the potential to go anywhere he wants.'" [xiv]

After the breakout game against Gavilan in week 4, Allen averaged 316.8 passing yards per game. In the team's final eight games, he tossed 26 touchdowns and ran for nine more. He had three 100-yard rushing games that season, displaying dual-threat ability. [xiv]

Rodriguez knew that, unfortunately, Allen was a short-term quarterback. After that performance against Merced, offers would start coming in, and Allen was going to be on his way to play Division I football. But

Rodriguez and Allen were both surprised at the lack of interest.

Again, Allen was going forgotten. Fresno State continued to turn their back on him, and Indiana offered him a scholarship and then pulled it. Eastern Michigan showed interest but never offered him a scholarship. Only Wyoming stepped in and offered Allen a full scholarship, and Allen, as expected, accepted it.

It was Wyoming Cowboys' assistant David Brown who started the wheels in motion. The Cowboys had just lost out on winning Eric Dungey, who turned Wyoming down to go to Syracuse at the last minute. Brown had seen Allen at Reedley and was impressed. He informed offensive coordinator Brent Vigen to take a look at this kid Allen and consider recruiting him after the Dungey offer blew up. Vigen loved what he saw, and within a week, Allen committed to Wyoming after the first semester ended.

What made Allen's year more special was just how he overcame an awful start to make something of it. Through his first two games, he came off the bench and played horribly. He wanted to be the guy, but he knew to be that guy, he had to be patient and not try to make too much happen. Reedley believed in him, finally started him despite his early struggles, and Allen took off.

"I think the biggest adjustment he had to make was, I'll be very honest with you, was the fact that he was the starter pretty much throughout his whole high school career, and he didn't start right away," Rodriguez said. "And I remember him just asking me, 'Coach, I'm ready. I'm ready.'" xiv

According to Rodriguez, the other players loved him. He got along with everyone, and the other quarterbacks looked up to him. He developed a great connection with Rafael Araujo-Lopes, who went to Pittsburgh and was a star receiver for the Panthers.

"He's a high character kid," Rodriguez said. "Always positive. He was always very positive and upbeat and trying to lift their spirits up and just being a great teammate." [xiv]

Allen threw for 2,055 yards, 26 touchdowns, and five interceptions in his one year at Reedley. He also rushed 120 times for 660 yards and ten touchdowns. Wyoming was excited to get him and develop him. [xiv]

Wyoming

After the last two seasons at Firebaugh and his season at Reedley, Josh Allen was used to being the star quarterback. But he would have to wait before he got to show his skills at Wyoming.

Allen was considered a redshirt freshman since it was his first year at the FCS level. His year at Reedley did not count as eligibility towards Division I.

He learned behind Cameron Coffman and Nick Smith in training camp. Coffman, a senior, set an all-time record at Wyoming in 2012 for most passing yards there as a freshman. But an injury early his sophomore season sidelined him for two years. He finally got his chance to start again during his senior year and threw for 1,981 yards.

Before he came back, Smith started, but the plan was to let Allen ease into action. Allen played a little bit his first game and came in his second game against Eastern Michigan. But after just two passes, Allen broke his collarbone, ending his 2015 season early.

Allen would spend the season learning as he had to sit out. When he came back healthy for spring camp, Allen was far and away the best quarterback on the roster. The Cowboys committed to Allen as quarterback after watching him grow incredibly before starting his sophomore year. According to Vigen, he was filling out his frame and chucking passes some 80 yards in practice.

Another significant impact for Allen was the hiring of Craig Bohl from North Dakota State during the 2014 season. Bohl had an excellent reputation as an offensive coach, helping to lead the Bison to four straight national championships. He also had recruited Carson Wentz out of high school. He immediately connected with Allen and helped him reach his potential during the 2016 season.

Before Allen coming in and starting, the Cowboys had a disastrous history. They finished 2015 with a woeful 2-10 record. Their last winning season came in 2011. Since 2000, they had just three winning seasons. Bohl and Allen had a big challenge in not only getting the program on the winning track for the first in a long time but also maintaining it. The Cowboys had not had back-to-back winning seasons since the 1990s. Bohl struggled in his first two years, playing with old recruits, but once he got his recruits in there, one of those being Allen, Wyoming had promise for the future.

In his first game starting for the Cowboys, Wyoming faced a dangerous opponent in Northern Illinois. But Allen was efficient and composed, leading the Cowboys down the field and made big plays in helping them get to overtime. Then in triple overtime with the game tied at 34, Allen scrambled and weaved around defenders, moving side to side before darting forward and running 22 yards and lunging across the goal line for the game-winning score. 40-34 Wyoming. Because of a lengthy rain delay to start the game, the game did not end until 2:34 a.m. local time. [xv]

Allen threw 19 completions in the game for 245 yards, two touchdowns, and no picks. He left with an efficiency rating of 159.2. Allen also rushed ten times for 70 yards and a touchdown. Not a bad way to start your career as the team's number one guy.

"The last play, it was amazing, but I kind of expect amazing from One Seven," running back Brian Hill said afterward. "He's just got that talent. He's got that 'it' factor. It's not a lot of people who have all the confidence in the world and can go throw the ball 80 yards. He has all the tools, and he's putting them together great." xv

As expected, Allen struggled against a much superior opponent in Nebraska. The Cornhuskers were just better in almost every position and frustrated Allen. Their defensive line broke through and gave Allen no time to throw. Allen threw five interceptions as opposed to just one touchdown as the Cornhuskers routed Wyoming 52-17 in what would be one of Allen's worst games of his career. Four of Allen's picks came in the final quarter, and when the time came to evaluate him as a pro prospect, scouts would use that game against him.

That game would be a blip on the radar by the end of the season as Allen never saw stats anywhere close to that game. He rallied with a three-touchdown performance the following week and a near-perfect 250.2 efficiency rating.

Allen would continually mature as the season progressed. The Cowboys were also aided by running back Brian Hill, who had career games against Eastern Michigan and Colorado State. After getting off to a 3-2 start, the Cowboys faced Air Force at home, one of their more formidable opponents that season.

Allen displayed his arm strength in the game, once again connecting on long passes throughout the game. He was never one to complete 40 or 50 passes a game. Bohl had a reputation for being a balanced coach. But when Allen completed a pass, it was usually a big one.

That game, Allen completed 15 passes for 173 yards but tossed touchdown passes of 17, 20, and 32 yards to help lift Wyoming over Air Force. Allen and Hill also were dynamic with the spread option. Hill ran for 92 yards and a score while Allen carried it 13 times for 74 yards.

One of the highlights of Allen's season came against number 13-ranked Boise State. The Cowboys were obvious underdogs and hadn't beaten a top-25 team in 14 years. Boise State had aspirations to put themselves in position for a potential playoff berth at the end of the year and entered the game 7-0.

Allen had already thrown two touchdowns when he took possession in the fourth quarter, the Cowboys trailing 28-21. Allen led them down to the 27-yard line. In what would be called Allen's favorite throw of the year, he rolled to his right and out of traffic, heaved a pass to the back of the end zone for Tanner Gentry, and put it perfectly in his arms for a touchdown to tie the game.

Incredibly, with just under two minutes left, Wyoming pinned Boise State back inside the five and sacked quarter Brett Rypien for the game-winning safety.

Wyoming stunned Boise State 30-28 and improved to 6-2. Allen threw three touchdowns that game. [xv]

Allen's incredible momentum carried through into the following week. Against Utah State, another solid team in the conference, Allen and the Cowboys threw all over their defense in the first half. Just before halftime, Allen dodged a blitz and rolled to his right. With nowhere to go, he began rolling over to his left. Running out of room, he found a slight hole in the pocket to step into and then flung a pass deep from his side of the field. The ball flew some 50 or 60 yards into the back of the end zone and into the hands of a diving Gentry for a touchdown. [xv]

The play would be one of the top plays of the week in college football. It also capped off a 35-point half for the Cowboys. Allen threw four touchdowns in the game and left with a 189 efficiency rating in a 52-28 rout over Utah State.

After reaching 7-2 for the first time in over 20 years, Wyoming hit a skid at the end of the season, losing four of their last five, including a bowl game. Allen's numbers were still good, throwing four touchdowns against UNLV in a loss, two in a win over San Diego State, and then three in a loss to San Diego State in the conference title game.

Wyoming would go to the Poinsettia Bowl that year and play BYU. Trailing 24-7, Allen lead a charge in the fourth quarter, throwing two touchdown passes to Genry to cut the Cougars' lead to 24-21. But they could not rally all the way, and the score stood as BYU won the bowl game. Wyoming still finished the year 8-6, their first winning season since 2011.

For Allen, he finished the year throwing for 3,203 yards and 28 touchdowns, achieving a 144.9 passer rating. He also ran 142 times for 523 yards and seven touchdowns. He even caught a touchdown on a trick play that season. Allen was a crucial contributor in the

Cowboys scoring 35.9 points per game and ranking number 25 in the country in scoring offense. He led all of the Mountain West in touchdowns and was number 20 in the country. [xvi]

With 3,276 total yards that season, he ranked third all-time in Wyoming history. His 36 total touchdowns would rank second all-time in Cowboys history. [xvi]

2017 Season

Josh Allen's 2016 season had gained national attention, and going into 2017, some murmurs about his NFL potential began to circulate. Per the NCAA rules, redshirt sophomores were eligible, and Allen had three years of playing experience. With Brian Hill going pro, Allen contemplated it as well. Some NFL scouts had him getting drafted in the first round despite not many people knowing who he was.

Reviews were mixed on Allen. Most questioned the competition he faced and looked at the Nebraska game as a concern. But Allen's size and arm strength could not be overlooked. He continued to fill out his frame, and his ability to hit long passes on the button was impressive. He was also mobile, maybe not to the level of Lamar Jackson and Kyler Murray, but he knew how to get big chunks of yards with his legs. He ran the spread offense to perfection in Wyoming.

Allen went to San Diego to train for the upcoming NFL Draft, although he never committed. He was still thinking about it and leaning towards going pro. But in early January, he had a change of heart. He talked to Craig Bohl, the coaches, and his family, and on January 12, announced that he was staying in Laramie to play another season for the Cowboys.

Allen was somewhat inspired by Carson Wentz, another quarterback from a small college and under his head coach, Craig Bohl. Wentz talked to Allen over the phone while Allen was trying to decide whether to go pro or not.

"You're 20 years old," Wentz told Allen. "You're stepping into a locker room with 30 and 35-year-old dudes with wives and kids, and they're counting on you to make plays and win games. If you're not ready for that, it'll eat you up." [xvii]

According to Allen, Wentz was sincere and very real about what the NFL was like. He just was not quite ready for it and wanted one more year of experience.

"I was very close to being an NFL player, and that's the only thing I've ever wanted to do growing up," Allen said. "At the same time, you're thinking about what you want to do for the rest of your life or the next 15, 20 years, and being ready. Sometimes they don't gel, and people make the decision to go early, and they don't end up in the league for more than four years. I looked upon that and said, 'I want to have a 15-year career in the NFL, and to come back for one more year is not going to hurt my chances.'" [xvii]

The fact that Allen wasn't ready made it the right move to return. After the 2017 season, he would likely be more prepared and ready to make the jump. Making that leap is such a big one, and you need to be 100% ready.

Some would say Allen's 2017 season wasn't as great as 2016. He played in only 11 games compared to 14 that season and threw 12 fewer touchdown passes. His yards per game were also way down. Some of it had to do with a lot of talent leaving Wyoming. But Allen still found ways to make plays and win games, leading the Cowboys to their first back-to-back winning seasons since the 1990s.

Allen struggled again against stiffer competition when he faced Iowa in the first game of the season. Allen had solid numbers, going 23-for-40 for 174 yards, but threw no touchdowns and two picks in a 24-3 opening day loss. Once again, the Allen critics pointed to a bad game against stiffer competition, something that they would use against him when sizing him up against other quarterbacks in the Draft.

Allen recovered the following week throwing two touchdowns against Gardner-Webb in a win. His best game would come later in the season against New Mexico.

Entering the game 4-3, Allen and the Cowboys' offense dominated New Mexico in every facet. Allen threw 16 completions that day for 234 yards and four touchdowns. Allen also ran for 20 yards and a score in the game and finished with a 174.5 efficiency rating, his second-highest of the season. Allen would be named Mountain West Conference Player of the Week for his five-touchdown performance.

Allen finished his career close to home in the Potato Idaho Bowl in Boise against Central Michigan. Allen and the offense exploded from the start. Allen first hit Jared Scott for a 23-yard touchdown in the opening minutes of the game. Just a couple of minutes later, he connected with Austin Conway from 11 yards out. Later that quarter, Allen threw a laser to C.J. Johnson from 45 yards out to give Wyoming a 21-7 lead before the first 15 minutes were even up.

Wyoming would go on to win the Idaho Bowl 37-14 in what would be Allen's final game as a Wyoming Cowboy. He was awarded the Most Valuable Player of the bowl game. Allen would finish the season throwing for 1,812 yards and 16 touchdowns through the air. He also ran for 204 yards and five scores.

After the game, Allen told reporters he would take a few days to consider his next move. But everyone knew what the answer would be.

Josh Allen was headed to the NFL.

Chapter 4: NFL Career

The 2018 NFL Draft was rich with quarterbacks. Along with Josh Allen, there was Baker Mayfield, Sam Darnold, Josh Rosen, and Lamar Jackson. At least three of those players were all but guaranteed to go within the first seven or eight picks.

Allen's positives were tough to ignore, per the scouting reports. Some said that he had one of the best arms in the game. He was big and strong and could throw the ball in tight windows and make head-scratching throws. He was also mobile and could extend plays with his legs. [xviii]

Among the negatives was his completion percentage at Wyoming against weak competition, completing just 56 percent of his passes. Some scouts also questioned his decision-making and said that his passes on crossing routes tend to get away from him. [xviii]

At the NFL Combine, Allen displayed solid results. He ran the 40-yard dash in 4.75 seconds and displayed a hand size over ten inches, quite large for a quarterback. On Pro Days, he answered many of the negatives in his scouting reports and shot up draft boards, and looked to be a top ten lock.

The Browns, as expected, used their top pick to draft Baker Mayfield. Many thought that the Jets would select Allen with the third pick overall. However, they passed on him and instead drafted USC quarterback Sam Darnold, a current member of the Carolina Panthers.

The Tampa Bay Buccaneers had the seventh pick, but the Buffalo Bills called them to make a trade. The Bills were in love with Josh Allen and were willing to give up their two second-round picks to obtain him. The Bucs agreed to the trade, and Buffalo selected Allen to be the franchise's new future.

Buffalo got one of their second-round picks back when they agreed to trade Sammy Watkins to the Kansas

City Chiefs. Watkins was the first-round pick back in 2014 but had failed to live up to expectations.

Some saw it as a gamble for the Bills. They pointed to Allen's 56 percent completion percentage at Wyoming as a sign that the Bills drafted a bust. They thought that Allen was wildly inaccurate, only making big plays against weak competition. However, when he faced teams like Oregon and Iowa, he collapsed.

But the Bills loved what they saw. According to general manager Brandon Beane, Josh was always number one on their board. They liked him better than Darnold and even Mayfield. He was worth it to move up and get. When they visited Josh and saw him work out, there was no doubt in their mind he would work out in Buffalo.

"When we left Laramie, we felt really good about Josh," Beane said. [v]

According to an article on ESPN, one football guru said, "Every piece of empirical evidence we have on

Allen leads him to being a failure." Dan Orlovsky also questioned whether he had the tools mentally to ever compete as a starting quarterback. [xix]

Hall of Famer Troy Aikman doubted him, saying his inaccuracy is a primary concern and that in 17 years studying the game, he never saw a bigger question mark in that area than Allen. The worst mockery may have come from an editor from NBC's Pro Football Talk.

"Roger Staubach is more accurate at 76 than Allen is now," they joked. [xix]

It seemed like everyone but the Buffalo Bills thought that Allen was going to be an epic bust. The Bills wasted their time moving up to draft someone who would not be in the league in ten years.

Allen heard it all, but unlike some quarterbacks, he didn't shy away from it. He wanted to read all the press clippings of reporters and so-called "experts" calling him a bust and a joke. He wanted to use it as fuel to succeed. It lit a fire inside him.

Not all experts, though, thought Allen would be a bust. Mel Kiper, Jr. was one of the scouts high on Allen. "His analytics weren't to the level that some want," Kiper said. "But that's why I call them ana-*lie*-tics. To me, you have to look deeper. A lot of his misses happened when they were down late in games and he was trying to make something happen. Yes, he got sloppy with his mechanics, but he also didn't take the easy five-yard throws that were going to come easy for him." [xix]

Kiper credited Allen's mentality, saying how good he gets along with teammates and how he never quits. Kiper also raved about how far he came, and sometimes the guys that travel the most distance from the bottom up have the most to gain.

One thing that experts didn't take into account was just how big of an underdog Allen was already and how far he's come. Just how hard of a worker Allen is and how he connects with his teammates. Those things couldn't be forgotten. Despite all of the stats they want to look at, Allen had the leadership, work ethic, and mentality to prove everyone wrong.

Rookie Season

Some rookies come out and are electric from the start. Carson Wentz was an MVP contender in his rookie season before he got hurt. Baker Mayfield broke rookie records in Cleveland. Dak Prescott made everyone forget about Tony Romo quickly in Dallas. Russell Wilson proved all doubters wrong from the start.

But Josh Allen was not in that camp. For Allen, he only gave his critics even more reason to bash him after his rookie season. It was difficult, although Allen was hardly to blame for many of the Buffalo Bills' problems. They lacked any weapons around him. Their top receiver was Zay Jones, a guy no one heard of, and their running back LeSean McCoy was old and a shell of his former self.

While Allen did not open the season as the starter, it only took one game for him to claim that title. Allen and Buffalo were outplayed in every aspect of the game on Opening Day 2018. Baltimore completely dominated Buffalo from the opening whistle. By halftime, it was 26-0, and the Bills had already benched Nathan Peterman.

Peterman could not get any first downs and put up horrible numbers, forcing the Bills to turn to Allen. Allen did not fare much better the rest of the game, completing just six passes for 74 yards. He was sacked three times and threw for just five first downs. He achieved a terrible efficiency rating of just 56.0. It was an all-around embarrassing opening game. The Ravens won 47-3.

In Allen's first home game in Week 2, he got his first-ever start and faced off against the Chargers and saw some success. Unfortunately, he had a lot of bad moments as well. Allen had a dreadful first half, throwing two interceptions, and the Bills trailed 28-6 at halftime. Allen bounced back a little in the second half and threw his first touchdown pass just before the game ended to cut the Chargers' victory to 31-20. But Allen again had a poor efficiency rating of just 61.3.

Through his first six games, Allen had a 2-4 record, throwing just two touchdown passes as opposed to five interceptions. He had some good moments, the best being the Bills' upset win in Minnesota as a 14-point underdog, where he achieved a 111.0 rating and 68 percent completion rating. But there was too much inconsistency, and many thought he was not ready for the spotlight yet.

After a tough performance against the Texans in Week 6, Allen left in the fourth quarter with an elbow injury that would keep him out for several weeks. When Nathan Peterman replaced him, the results were just as dreadful. Buffalo went 1-3 under Peterman, and by the time he was back healthy and ready to start, the Bills were 3-7.

While pundits got on the Bills and Allen, there was just no talent around him. The offensive line was a major problem. Allen was sacked 21 times in his first six games, included a seven-sack game against the Packers. There was no threat at running back with LeSean McCoy and Chris Ivory splitting time and neither hitting 100 yards in a game. At wide receiver, they had nothing. Their top receivers, Zay Jones and Robert Foster, would have difficulty making most teams' rosters.

Allen's legs, though, were a positive. He led the Bills in rushing in 2018. When he returned from his injury, there was a clear change in Buffalo's philosophy of letting Allen use his legs more. Against the Jaguars, he ran for 99 yards and a score. The following week against Miami, he ran for 135 yards. Then the next week against the Jets, he ran for 101 yards and a touchdown.

In fact, through Allen's first nine games, he had five passing touchdowns and five rushing touchdowns. There was notably some progress in Allen, although it did not show too much in the wins column. With three games left in the season, the Bills were sitting at 5-7, most of it behind their strong defense, which had gotten them to the postseason the year before.

In the final game of the year, Allen gave the fans of Buffalo some hope. Playing at home against the Dolphins, Allen broke out and made some huge plays with his arm. He opened the game with an 80-yard drive that resulted in a one-yard scramble and touchdown run. Then just two minutes later, he hit Jones from 18 yards out to give the Bills an early 14-0 lead.

In the second half, Allen his Foster from 5 yards out to give the Bills a 21-14 lead. Leading 28-17 in the fourth,

Allen lined up from Miami's 30-yard line, avoided a blitz, and stepped up into the pocket, and then took off. He scrambled 30 yards and past Miami defenders for his second rushing touchdown of the game. A few minutes after that, he hit Jones for the second time that game, this time a 26-yard touchdown pass for a 42-17 lead and win.

It was by far Allen's best game of the year. He totaled five touchdowns, three through the air and two on the ground. He threw for 224 yards and ran for 95 more. The 114.9 efficiency rating was his best yet as a Buffalo Bill.

Allen finished the year throwing for 2,074 yards in 12 games. He threw ten touchdowns but also 12 picks and achieved a 53 percent completion rating. On the ground, he took off 89 times for 631 yards and eight touchdowns.

Allen's first season could be described as bumpy but promising. For most rookie quarterbacks, you want to see progression and hope. Allen gave that to Bills fans by the end of the season. That final game against Miami gave the team something to look forward to in their first-round draft pick. Allen wanted more weapons, though, around him. That opening season, he showed some big play potential, which showed in him finishing number eight among all quarterbacks in yards per completion. He also had three-game winning drives.

Among quarterbacks in 2018, Allen led them all in rushing with 52.6 yards per game, the best among all starters. His eight rushing touchdowns were also the best among all quarterbacks and number 14 among all rushers in the NFL that year.

The Bills worked on getting Allen some help around him in the offseason. They added veteran receivers John Brown and Cole Beasley and drafted running back Devin Singletary after releasing both Ivory and McCoy.

More than anything, they began to believe Allen. The critics may still have not believed yet, but the organization was starting to.

2019 Season

Expectations were higher on Josh Allen in 2019. The question was whether he could help take the Bills to the postseason and finally past the New England Patriots in the AFC East, something that no other AFC East team had done in the Brady era.

Buffalo started 2019 much better than they had in 2018. While Allen was not playing like Tom Brady, he was efficient and balanced. When he needed to make plays early in the season, he made them. The Bills defense played their part, and through three games of the 2019 season, Allen and the Bills were 3-0 and atop the division.

Allen's numbers were mixed. He continued to use his legs, scoring two touchdowns on the ground, but he was also making plays through the air. Through three games, he was averaging 250 yards per game and had thrown for three scores. But Allen also made mistakes, had three picks, and lost two fumbles.

According to Allen, the turning point in his career came after Week 4 against the Patriots. Allen put up a dud when playing at home against the Super Bowl champions and trying to take the AFC East honor away from the dynasty. The Bills offense could not get anything going. Defensively, they hung in the game, but they couldn't muster up many points. [ii]

It was Allen's worst game of his career. He threw three interceptions and no touchdowns. He compiled just a 24.0 efficiency rating, going 13-for-28 for just 153 yards in the 16-10 loss. [ii]

The media got on Josh Allen for his performance. Allen had thrown three touchdowns and six interceptions in those first four games. Many quarterbacks would have crumbled after that type of performance with their confidence shaken.

But something happened to Josh after that game. The rest of the season, Allen threw 17 touchdowns and just three interceptions. His best game came against Miami in Week 11. There, Allen threw 21 completions on 33 attempts for 256 yards and three touchdowns. He also rushed for 56 yards and a score. [iii]

In his second year, Allen was not Patrick Mahomes, putting up MVP numbers and wowing teams with his stats, but he was a symbol of progress. A year before, he struggled to get 200 yards in a game and was throwing more picks than touchdowns. As 2019 progressed, Allen was a different quarterback, particularly after the Patriots game. He was maturing and becoming a leader in the Bills offense. He was not an overnight sensation, but he was steadily getting better. Part of the reason for that was offensive coordinator Brian Daboll.

"A lot of the credit for Josh's progression should go to Brian (Daboll)," Mel Kiper said. "He has given Josh the confidence, the latitude to go out and run the team the way he sees it in conjunction with the plays he's calling. He's worked to develop Josh into a quarterback who can take shots deep but also be patient enough to keep the chains moving. I think Daboll is going to get a head-coaching job because of what he's done with Josh, and the whole town of Buffalo is made for Josh." xix

Allen produced a 10-6 season for the Bills and took them to their second playoff appearance in three years. They were not good enough to overtake New England for the division, but they had made a lot of progress from throughout the year and were nipping at their heels.

Allen ended the 2019 season with 3,029 yards and 20 touchdowns as opposed to nine interceptions. He continued to be a threat on the ground, rushing 109 times for 510 yards. Allen finished the season third among all quarterbacks in rushing behind only the speedy Lamar Jackson and Kyler Murray. However, he finished eighth among all rushers in touchdowns and first among quarterbacks in rushing scores. [ii]

Allen helped get the Bills to the postseason in Houston against Deshaun Watson and the Texans, but despite getting out to a 16-0 lead, the Bills let the Texans back in it. The Texans tied the game and then won it in overtime, sending Buffalo home early in the playoffs.

Allen's first postseason game was not his best. He completed 24 of 46 passes for 264 yards and no scores. He was also sacked three times and lost a crucial fumble.

Despite a disappointing finish, the 2019 season had to be hailed as a success for Allen. He had continued to develop, and after a woeful game against New England in Week 4, went on a stretch over the last 12 games that was one of the best in the NFL. He was maturing and just needed more weapons around him.

"I think the big gap from his first to second year was anticipation, throwing with more anticipation, which is where I think he grew a ton," Jordan Palmer said, Allen's quarterback coach. I think the theme for this year will be the deep ball because it was well-documented (that he struggled in that area), controlling that. So based off what I've seen the last few years, I would just assume that he's going to come back and be one of the best deep-ball throwers in the league next year. I see the way that he addresses issues and moves on." [xxi]

In the offseason, the Bills got Allen a huge weapon that would help set the team up to take another step forward in 2020: Stefon Diggs.

2020 Season

With Tom Brady leaving New England to go to Tampa Bay, the Bills instantly became the favorite to win the AFC East, especially after the addition of Stefon Diggs on offense. Diggs cost the Bills a first-round pick, the

22nd pick, but they felt it was worth it and that Diggs could be the missing ingredient to their lack of weapons around Allen.

Diggs instantly connected with Allen despite not practicing with him because of the COVID-19 pandemic in the 2020 offseason. But the two spent a lot of time getting to know each other over the phone and video games, playing Call of Duty through a headset. Eventually, the two would get together and hang out and start practicing together as the season got closer, but it would not be until August.

When the two of them did start playing together, it did not take long for them to get on the same page, even without a preseason. The two had great respect for each other, and it led to great results from the start. The Bills would win their first four games, starting 4-0 for the first time since the Jim Kelly days.

Allen was a big part of the reason for the great start. Until 2020, when you thought of Allen, you thought of a 200 to 250-yard game, a couple touchdowns, and maybe a pick with some rushing success. Through four games, Allen was averaging well over 300 yards per game and had thrown ten touchdowns as opposed to just one pick. Oh yeah, and he was still rushing for success, scoring three times with his legs.

This was a completely different quarterback. He had developed the way he knew he could, and critics of Allen began to wither away fast. Allen started the season with a 312-yard performance in a win against the Jets. Then he led an offensive assault on the Dolphins, throwing for 415 yards and four touchdowns in a 31-28 victory. He threw four more touchdowns the following week in a 311-yard performance and win against the Los Angeles Rams.

Three key areas were adding to Allen's success. First, the offensive line had been much improved. Allen was not getting touched nearly as much as he had in past seasons. Secondly, Diggs was the apparent missing piece in the receiving game, and his presence allowed receivers like John Brown and Cole Beasley to get more open and make plays. Third, Allen gained confidence in himself and was having fun out there, a key ingredient to success.

"I don't know the past. I just know Josh right now, and he's playing great football," Diggs said. "I feel like we're scratching the surface on the potential we have." xxi

With the Patriots not the same team without Brady and starting off the season out slow, the Bills were the team to beat now in the AFC East, poised to end the Patriots' reign as champions.

"Each week, it's gotten a little better," Daboll said. "We kind of feel we know who we are right now." xxi

The Bills, however, hit a snag in Weeks 5 and 6 against brutal competition. First, they were run over by Derrick Henry and the Titans in Nashville, who shredded the Bills' defense and dominated in a 42-16 win. Then in the heavy rain at Orchard Park on a rare Monday Night late afternoon start because of a coronavirus rescheduling, Allen struggled against the Chiefs. He completed just half of his passes and threw a pick in a 26-17 loss. [ii]

Some thought the Bills season was already imploding. After all, Buffalo fans had seen this song and dance before. But after that Kansas City loss, the Bills season turned back around. They won nine of them over their last ten games and their only loss came on a miracle play.

The Bills beat the Jets, Patriots, and Seahawks to move to 7-2 on the year. In those three games, Allen was average, throwing three touchdowns and just one interception. However, Allen ran for two scores. The offense broke out in a big way in a showdown at home against the Seahawks. The Bills got out to an early 24-7 lead and hung on late to win 44-34 in what some thought could be an early Super Bowl preview. Allen threw two touchdowns and racked up a 138.5 efficiency rating. [ii]

Perhaps the worst loss of the year came against Arizona. Trailing 26-23, Allen led the Bills on a game-winning drive in the final two minutes. With 34 seconds left, Allen connected with Diggs from 21 yards out to give the Bills the apparent victory, 30-26.

However, Arizona took three plays and got it down to the Buffalo 43 with just two seconds left. Kyler Murray heaved a Hail Mary pass into the end zone and the great DeAndre Hopkins outleaped everyone and came down with it for a touchdown. The Cardinals beat the Bills 32-30, erasing an incredible performance from Allen where he led the Bills from behind. [ii]

But the Bills would rack off six consecutive wins, putting that game well behind them. In San Francisco, Allen threw four touchdowns and threw 375 yards in a win that got the Bills to 9-3 and on the verge of the AFC East title.

Then on a Sunday night in Pittsburgh, Allen rallied his team from behind and vaulted Buffalo into the playoffs with a 26-15 win.

The following week against the Broncos, Allen exploded. He threw for 359 yards and two touchdowns while also rushing two touchdowns. But it was the types of throws that Allen made that stunned people. He completed several long passes right on the money and threaded the needle on other throws. He was 28 of 40 in what Jordan Palmer called one of the best games he had ever seen from the quarterback. The Bills dominated Denver in the first half and got to sit most of their starters in the second half as they officially clinched the AFC East title with a 48-19 win, becoming the first time not named the Patriots to win the AFC East in over ten years.

"I told Josh I think he just made three of the best throws I'd ever seen in my life," Beasley told me after the Bills' 49-19 Week 15 win over Denver. "When you're playing with a guy like that, it drives you to get open every play because you know he's going to find you." [xx]

The Bills played their starters their final two games because they had an opportunity to clinch home-field advantage. They dominated New England and Miami. Allen, who had always struggled against the Patriots, finally found his rhythm, connecting for four touchdowns with his receivers and throwing for 320 yards. Then against Miami, Allen threw three more touchdowns as the Bills completed a 13-3 season with a 56-26 win. The Chiefs' win gave them the top seed in the AFC with the Bills right behind them.

Allen's progression continued. For the third straight year, he saw improvement with his numbers. He finished the year with 4,544 yards passing, 37 touchdowns, and just ten interceptions. He also ran for 421 yards and eight touchdowns, making it a combined 45 scores in 2020.

Although it was canceled due to the COVID-19 pandemic, Allen was voted to the Pro Bowl and was a clear candidate alongside Aaron Rodgers for Most Valuable Player. Allen was near or at the top in nearly every statistical category at the end of that season. He was fifth in total yards, fifth in touchdowns, fourth in completion percentage (69.2), fourth in first downs (242), sixth in yards per game (284), third in quarterback rating (81.7), and fifth in total completions (396).

Allen received four first-place votes in the MVP race, finishing ahead of Patrick Mahomes for second place but well behind Aaron Rodgers for first. What was most important for Allen, though, wasn't the hardware. It was winning the Super Bowl. The Bills had a chance at their first one ever behind Allen.

2020 Postseason

It had been a long time since the Bills hosted a playoff game. Traditionally, the Bills would have a first-round bye as the number two seed. But because the NFL playoffs expanded to 14 teams, the second seed would have to play a Wild Card Game. It would not be an easy one, either, as the Indianapolis Colts had shown during the season that they could play with and beat anyone.

It looked as if Buffalo was on their way to the Divisional Round after Josh Allen connected with Stefon Diggs on a beautiful touchdown pass to start the fourth quarter that put the Bills ahead 24-10. But the Colts fought back. Trailing 27-17 late in the game, Philip Rivers led his team down the field's length and hit Jack Doyle from 27 yards out to cut the game to three. [xxii]

For most of the game, the Bills had been in command, but it was slipping out of control late, especially when they failed to convert a critical third down and handed the ball back over to Indianapolis. The Colts now had a chance to drive down the field and either tie it or win it.

However, the Bills' defense stepped up big in the final minute. From the 47, Rivers tried one last heave to the end zone to try and win the game, but the ball was batted down, and the Bills hung on to win, 27-24. [xxii]

For the first time in 25 years, the Bills had won a playoff game.

"Obviously, we started off a little slow and were able to get into a little bit of rhythm late," Allen said. "It's new territory for myself, but it gives us a chance to play next week." [xxii]

Allen finished the game throwing for 324 yards and two touchdowns and an efficiency rating of 121.6. He also ran for 54 yards and a score. It was a much better performance this his first playoff game against the Texans a year ago. [xxii]

It was new territory. Allen never experienced the playoffs in college at a school like Wyoming. In high school, they went to the playoffs but never went anywhere. For the first time, he was chasing a championship and wanted it. But the next game wouldn't be easy against the Baltimore Ravens, who ended the season one of the hottest teams in the league.

It was a primetime Saturday night game in freezing cold Buffalo. It also was a game where both offenses didn't do anything. Most of the drama came in the third period. With the game tied at 3, Allen connected with Stefon Diggs from three yards out to break the tie and give Buffalo a 10-3 lead.

It appeared, however, that Baltimore would tie the game as Lamar Jackson took the Ravens right down the field and inside the Bills' five-yard line. However, Taron Johnson picked off a Lamar Jackson pass in the end zone and saw nothing but green in front of him. He took it back 101 yards the other direction to completely turn the game from a potential 10-10 tie to a 17-3 Bills lead. Orchard Park went crazy.

That was all the fireworks in the game—no more scoring. Defenses ruled the night, and the Bills advanced to their first AFC Championship game in 26 years with a 17-3 win over the Ravens. Allen finished the game with 206 yards and a score, but most importantly, no turnovers.

The AFC Championship Game would be in Kansas City with the winner going to Tampa to play the Buccaneers, who beat the Packers in the NFC Championship Game earlier in the afternoon. For much of the week, the Bills didn't know who to prepare to play at quarterback. Patrick Mahomes had suffered a concussion in the team's win over the Browns and was in protocol most of the week. However, he was cleared by the weekend, and the Bills knew to be the beat, they'd have to beat the best. The Chiefs were the champs.

There would be hope early for Buffalo. A huge turnover deep by Kansas City was taken back nearly the other way. Allen hit Dawson Knox from three yards out to give the Bills a 9-0 lead midway through the first quarter. But after that, it was all Kansas City.

The Chiefs outscored the Bills 21-0 over the next ten minutes to break out a big lead. Allen played decently, but he could not make the big plays like he did most of the season. The Chiefs' offense was just unstoppable. Despite a couple of late touchdowns to make the score respectable, Kansas City had ended the Bills season with a 38-24 win in the AFC Championship. However, the Chiefs could not defend their title as they lost to the Bucs a couple of weeks later in Super Bowl LV, 31-9.

Still, for Allen, the story had changed. Before the season, there were doubts. After the season, Allen was recognized as one of the best quarterbacks in the game. Before the season, he was still growing into a leader. By the end of the season, he was a well-respected leader in the locker room. Before the season, the city liked him. After the season, they were in love with him.

So what changed with Josh Allen so much? How did he go from struggling in his rookie season to progressing and becoming a Pro Bowl quarterback? Getting extra help around him played a big role, as did experience in the game. According to his offensive coordinator, a big reason was that they changed the playbook to match Josh's strengths.

"From his first year to his second year, I think Josh had nine new guys starting around him," Daboll says. "We didn't add a ton this year, other than [Diggs]. But we're constantly evolving the offense to fit what he does best and what he feels most comfortable with. We tailor everything to Josh. And to be fair, he's been fortunate to have the same system and grow in that same system for three years. That's not always the case in this league. It takes a village to develop a young quarterback, but it starts with him." [xix]

Chapter 5: Personal Life

"He's real. He doesn't try to pretend to be something that he's not. He has a way of connecting to people from really all over. And he lays it on the line. He's a good listener. He's demanding of himself. ... This dude is Buffalo. He's got a chip on his shoulder." [xxiii]

- Brian Daboll, Bills offensive coordinator

Brian Daboll's quote says a lot about what Josh Allen is like personally, and you will hear nobody dispute his quote. Allen is a down-to-earth guy who people love to be around. When his grandmother passed away in November 2020, and the fans rallied around him to pledge money to the hospital that he helps out at, it spoke volumes about the love between Allen and Bills fans.

It's rare to see that outpouring of support for a football player. But Allen has proven his whole life that he is not a selfish person. He has spent his time helping others and being gracious to those around him.

"When he came in off the field and into the locker room, he kind of fell into my arms a little bit," Daboll said after Allen's grandmother passed. "A lot of emotion there, particularly for him, but for me also. When you love somebody, and something happens like that, it's tough. And to see it happen to somebody that you really care about as a player, that's tough. But that's why his teammates love him, too. All-day competitive. All-day tough. They'd do anything for him." *xxiii*

Josh Allen has never been a big city guy. Even though Buffalo is big, it's different than the New York City's and Chicago's of the world. It's considered closer-knit. Allen grew up in a small town in Firebaugh and lived on a farm. He only saw a big city when he traveled to San Francisco to watch the Giants play.

After that, it was off to Laramie, Wyoming, which has a population of just over 30,000. While it's bigger than

Firebaugh, it's also relatively small compared to most college towns and very close-knit.

Love Life

Josh Allen started dating Brittany Williams just before the 2018 NFL Draft, and the two have had an extremely close relationship since, although it's not sure if wedding bells are in the future. They both grew up in Firebaugh and attended high school near each other. Toward the end of Allen leaving Firebaugh, the two started talking more regularly and started dating and staying in touch. While they were not high school sweethearts, they became college sweethearts. [xxiv]

Williams was a cheerleader at Fresno State and has since moved on to become a Pilates instructor. She admitted growing up that she had a crush on Josh since they were eight years old. If there's any doubt about how the two are going, there are constant updates on Instagram of the two posing together and taking pictures, especially when they're on vacation. The two recently visited Monaco and saw the Grand Prix there.

"Monaco, you have my heart," Williams posted on Instagram. "The most incredible trip of my life, followed by making so many incredible new friends and memories. Can't wait to go back already ♥□ #joshlovespix." [xxiv]

Williams currently works with the Conor J. Long Foundation in her Pilates class to help vault her career. According to a recent statement, "The Conor J. Long Foundation is excited to partner with Pilates Instructor Brittany Williams to provide a program for all ages that practices mindfulness. Over the next month, this program will be constructed to relax the body and mind while lowering stress levels through Pilates." [xxiv]

Many familiar with the couple expect an engagement soon. Williams loves Buffalo and visiting Josh to watch him play, and it is clear from pictures that the two are deeply in love.

Charity Work

Josh Allen spends most of his time donating and helping out at the Oishei Children's Hospital. There, he visits sick patients who are struggling with confidence as their life is falling apart. Josh's goal is to help bring smiles to their faces, and he does that given his reputation in the city.

Allen is big on the number 17, as indicated by the number he's worn and the fact that fans donated $17 each to donate to the hospital when his grandmother died. Allen has regularly written $17,000 checks to the hospital and has become a symbol of generosity in the city. Allen said he loves donating and giving to those in need. He also loves seeing kids at practices and games and connecting with them.

"That's probably my favorite thing about the platform I have," Allen said. "A small gesture can change somebody's day. Any time I'm at training camp or out in the public, every kid out there I try to give them at least a high five or sign an autograph. I always looked up to professional athletes, and I've seen a couple before. Going to games and just wanting a high five (Allen smacks his hands together) … "I'm never going to wash my hand again!" I was that type of kid who loved sports." xxv

Thanks to the fans of Buffalo, donations at Oishei Hospital have topped $500,000, an incredible show of support for Allen and his family. "Words can't really describe how I feel, how my family feels," Allen told reporters the first time he had spoken since his grandmother's death became public. "Every time I call my parents and let them know the new number, they just start bawling all over again. And to know that people care and that so much good is coming out of a tough situation, it means the world to myself, it means the world to my family." vi

Allen is currently signed on with the Bills for four years and $21 million, including a $13.5 million signing bonus. He now has a net worth of $5 million. All of this money is only likely to go up after he elevated his play in 2020. He just needs to keep up the good play.

Allen has landed a couple of big endorsement deals that could make him big money down the road. Those include an agreement with Nike and New Era Cap. Allen also has contracts with Microsoft Surface, Hyundai, and Tommy Armour Golf.

There are some things about Josh that are not surprising while some things are. Since he joined Buffalo, he has become a huge chicken wing fan. After all, Buffalo is the home to Buffalo wings, and if you live there, you have to eat them. When he met with general manager Brandon Beane for the first time, it was at a chicken wing joint and became hooked ever since.

Maybe more on the surprising side is who Josh Allen's favorite artist is. Josh Allen has "Bieber Fever." Yes, he's a Justin Bieber fan. According to Josh Allen, everyone is a secret Justin Bieber fan and hides it. However, he's not afraid to hide. He shares it regularly with the world. [xxvii]

Josh is also a bit superstitious. He is big on even numbers, which is ironic since he wears the number 17. But according to Josh, whenever he listens to the television, the level has to be set on an even number. When he eats chicken wings, it has to be 8, 10, or 12, or another even number. When he does reps in the weight room, it has to be an even number. [xxvii]

Chapter 6: Legacy and Future

When it comes to comparisons in Buffalo, Josh Allen is repeatedly put side by side with the most famous quarterback in Bills history: Jim Kelly. Most would argue that Kelly was the only successful quarterback Buffalo has ever had, and Allen has the potential to be right up there with him.

Allen and Kelly came from two different backgrounds. Kelly was a superstar growing up. He came from an athletic family and played at a school where quarterbacks win Heisman Trophies, and national championships are common, at least in the 1980s and 1990s: The University of Miami. Many quarterbacks who went to Miami were drafted in the first round. It was the home of Bernie Kosar, Vinny Testaverde, and former Heisman Trophy winner Gino Torretta.

Allen, on the other hand, grew up without superstar status. He attended junior college and then played at

Wyoming, a school where no quarterback before Allen was ever taken before the fifth round.

But both Allen and Kelly landed in Buffalo, and through three seasons, both have very similar records. In Kelly's first season, he went 4-12 with the Bills, one win less than Allen, who went 5-11, despite both players not playing every game.

Both had mediocre seasons but exploded onto the scene in their third year. After a 6-6 record in his second season, Kelly went 12-4 his third year. Allen went 13-3 his third year.

In an era where passing is much more commonplace, Allen has already broken numerous records in Buffalo. Just three years into his career, Allen holds the franchise record for most passing touchdowns in a season with 37, most total touchdowns in a season with 45 (taking into account rushing), highest completion percentage in a season at 69.2 percent, and best quarterback and efficiency rating.

While most look at Allen as a passing threat in the future, he has made the record books for his legs. He is the only quarterback in NFL history with at least seven rushing touchdowns in his first three seasons. No, Lamar Jackson, Michael Vick, nor Cam Newton could do that.

Cam Newton is the only quarterback in NFL history with more rushing touchdowns than Josh Allen has had in his first three years. Newton had 26 through three seasons, while Allen has 25. Most would not use the term "fast" to describe Allen, but most would call him "football fast," meaning that he has quick feet and can dodge tackles and find the holes. He also isn't afraid to put his head down.

Already with 9,707 yards in his career, he is sixth all-time in Bills history. In 2021, he is expected to move into fourth place behind only Kelly, Joe Ferguson, and Jack Kemp. As long as he stays with Buffalo, he should easily break Kelly's record within the next eight or nine years. Kelly has just over 35,000 yards but was nowhere near Josh Allen after his first three years.

On a larger scale, Allen is among the NFL leaders all-time through three seasons in several categories. With 67 touchdown passes, he ranks sixth all-time for most yards in a quarterback's first three seasons. That's more than Matt Ryan, Cam Newton, and Matthew Stafford had. [xxviii]

With a 5.0 touchdown percentage, he is tied with Baker Mayfield and Peyton Manning through their first three seasons and above greats like Andrew Luck and Joe Namath. [xxviii]

Allen also ranks 12th all-time for quarterbacks in their first three seasons for quarterback rating at 90.4. That is better than Baker Mayfield, Andrew Luck, Peyton Manning, and Matthew Stafford. [xxviii]

All that said, while Allen ranks statistically among the greatest in NFL history thus far in his career, it does not mean anything to him. He wants to win games since that's what you're defined by. Aaron Rodgers, Drew Brees, and Dan Marino are three of the greatest statistical leaders of all time, but they have just two combined Super Bowl rings. They are not in the same sentence as Tom Brady, who has seven of them.

Allen wants to bring the first Super Bowl trophy to Buffalo in history and erase years of frustration in the city he loves. Jim Kelly got to the big game four straight times but could never break through.

"Stats are for losers," Allen said. "And the one thing I'd like to point out, while at Wyoming, we won games, and I definitely think that's how quarterbacks are judged in the NFL." xxix

Allen has already garnered so much respect. The tables have turned for all those like Troy Aikman, who doubted his potential in the NFL when he was drafted. People are holding him in a much different regard, and the critics are few and far between. Greg Cosell, whose opinion means a lot, is now an ESPN analyst and a huge part of NFL Films and its success. He said he sees a lot of John Elway in Josh Allen.

"Allen is a much bigger man than Elway. Allen is the most intriguing quarterback I have watched and evaluated in all my years at NFL Films. It would not surprise me at all if we soon call Allen the most physically gifted quarterback the league has ever seen. Stay tuned." xxx

One reason why many think Allen has a Hall of Fame career is his attitude. Not only is he big with a strong arm, but he is tough and an incredible leader. The other players on the team love him and look up to him, and Allen is not afraid of anything. He has already been through so much and has been told he'd never make it in the league. He is proving so many of them wrong already.

"I'm not going to bow down to anybody, not going to back away from anybody," Allen said. "If you didn't want to believe in me, that's OK, because I'll make a believer out of you." xxix

For Josh Allen and the Bills to get to that next level, they've got to find a way to get past the Chiefs, a team that has taken the AFC's throne the last couple of years. Patrick Mahomes is a great quarterback, and in the offseason, the Chiefs have only built themselves and gotten better.

But Buffalo is also growing and improving. Allen will have another year in the system in 2021, and the Bills continue to bolster their offensive line and get better defensively so they can stop Kansas City in the playoffs. It appears as if the AFC East is now the Bills' to lose. The next question is whether Allen can bring home a Lombardi Trophy to Buffalo.

Conclusion

Josh Allen's work ethic and leadership have led him to be the perfect role model for young athletes. He has also given them a great piece of advice that you don't need to be a legend growing up or go to some big Division I program to be a legend when you get older.

"I think that kids who are at smaller schools or don't have offers from big schools can look at my story and continue to work hard. I preach to them that it doesn't matter where you come from: it matters how you play and how you apply yourself." [xxix]

It's an excellent lesson for the youth today. So many give up because they think that their dreams are already over. Josh Allen's dream was to be a professional quarterback, yet not one university wanted him out of high school.

Did he give up? No.

Josh kept playing. He played for a junior college and even had an awful start in his first two games there. But he stayed confident, stayed strong, and kept working hard, and eventually, things got better from there. Even after junior college, only one university wanted him, and he made the best of that opportunity at a small school like Wyoming.

He was then doubted in the NFL Draft with many saying that his numbers were not good enough to make it in the NFL. He would flop. Yet here he is, now recognized as one of the best young players in the game today.

But it's not just about his talents. It's about who he is as a person. Stardom did not change Josh Allen. He is the same caring and giving person today as he was growing up. He loves connecting with kids and fans and loves to display a smile. He's the same person off the camera that he is on. Because of that, kids everywhere have a new face to look up to.

You may be a Bills fan, a Chiefs fan, or a Patriots fan. It should not matter. When Josh Allen suits up on Sunday, you should root for him even if you don't root for the team. He's one of the good guys in the game today.

"I know his parents and his family. I know how he was raised, and you just can't help but root for him," Daboll said. "We've spent a lot of time together the last three years, and he means much more to me than just a quarterback and a player. The relationship we have built is something special, and it always will be. I just care about him as a person. I feel very fortunate to coach him but also to have him as a friend." [xix]

That should tell you everything you need to know about the kind of player and person Josh Allen is.

Final Word/About the Author

I was born and raised in Norwalk, Connecticut. Growing up, I could often be found spending many nights watching basketball, soccer, and football matches with my father in the family living room. I love sports and everything that sports can embody. I believe that sports are one of the most genuine forms of competition, heart, and determination. I write my works to learn more about influential athletes in the hopes that from my writing, you the reader can walk away inspired to put in an equal if not greater amount of hard work and perseverance to pursue your goals. If you enjoyed *Josh Allen: The Inspiring Story of One of Football's Star Quarterbacks,* please leave a review! Also, you can read more of my works on *David Ortiz, Mike Trout, Bryce Harper, Jackie Robinson, Aaron Judge, Odell Beckham Jr., Bill Belichick, Serena Williams, Rafael Nadal, Roger Federer, Novak Djokovic, Richard Sherman, Andrew Luck, Rob Gronkowski, Brett Favre, Calvin Johnson, Drew*

Brees, J.J. Watt, Colin Kaepernick, Aaron Rodgers, Peyton Manning, Tom Brady, Russell Wilson, Odell Beckham Jr., Bill Belichick, Charles Barkley, Trae Young, Gregg Popovich, Pat Riley, John Wooden, Steve Kerr, Brad Stevens, Red Auerbach, Doc Rivers, Erik Spoelstra, Michael Jordan, LeBron James, Kyrie Irving, Klay Thompson, Stephen Curry, Kevin Durant, Russell Westbrook, Anthony Davis, Chris Paul, Blake Griffin, Kobe Bryant, Joakim Noah, Scottie Pippen, Carmelo Anthony, Kevin Love, Grant Hill, Tracy McGrady, Vince Carter, Patrick Ewing, Karl Malone, Tony Parker, Allen Iverson, Hakeem Olajuwon, Reggie Miller, Michael Carter-Williams, John Wall, James Harden, Tim Duncan, Steve Nash, Draymond Green, Kawhi Leonard, Dwyane Wade, Ray Allen, Pau Gasol, Dirk Nowitzki, Jimmy Butler, Paul Pierce, Manu Ginobili, Pete Maravich, Larry Bird, Kyle Lowry, Jason Kidd, David Robinson, LaMarcus Aldridge, Derrick Rose, Paul George, Kevin Garnett, Chris Paul, Marc Gasol, Yao Ming, Al Horford, Amar'e

Stoudemire, DeMar DeRozan, Isaiah Thomas, Kemba Walker, Chris Bosh, Andre Drummond, JJ Redick, DeMarcus Cousins, Wilt Chamberlain, Bradley Beal, Rudy Gobert, Aaron Gordon, Kristaps Porzingis, Nikola Vucevic, Andre Iguodala, Devin Booker, John Stockton, Jeremy Lin, Chris Paul, Pascal Siakam, Jayson Tatum, Gordon Hayward, Nikola Jokic, Bill Russell, Victor Oladipo, Luka Doncic, Ben Simmons, Shaquille O'Neal, Joel Embiid, Donovan Mitchell, Damian Lillard and *Giannis Antetokounmpo* in the Kindle Store. If you love football, check out my website at claytongeoffreys.com to join my exclusive list where I let you know about my latest books and give you lots of goodies.

Like what you read? Please leave a review!

I write because I love sharing the stories of influential athletes like Josh Allen with fantastic readers like you. My readers inspire me to write more so please do not hesitate to let me know what you thought by leaving a review! If you love books on life, sports, or productivity, check out my website at claytongeoffreys.com to join my exclusive list where I let you know about my latest books. Aside from being the first to hear about my latest releases, you can also download a free copy of *33 Life Lessons: Success Principles, Career Advice & Habits of Successful People*. See you there!

Clayton

References

[i]   Cottrell, Jenna. "Stefon Diggs on How He Feels About Josh Allen." *13Wham.* 11 Nov 2020.

[ii]   "Josh Allen Stats." *Pro-Football Reference.* Nd. Web.

[iii]   "Josh Allen College Stats." *Sports-Reference.* Nd. Web.

[iv]   Simmons, Myles. "Sean McDermott: Josh Allen Certainly Proved Himself and What He Can Do." *Pro Football Talk.* 26 Jan 2021. Web.

[v]   Maiorana, Sal. "Farm to First Round: Buffalo Bills Josh Allen's Long Strange Trip to the NFL." *The Democrat & Chronicle.* 21 Jul 2018. Web.

[vi]   McCarriston, Shanna. "Bills Fans Donate $1 Million to Children's Hospital in Honor of Josh Allen's Late Grandmother." *CBS Sports.* 28 Dec 2020. Web.

[vii]   Feldman, A.J. "Snub from Josh Allen's Childhood Inspires Him to Give Back." *RochesterFirst.com.* 28 Oct 2020. Web.

[viii] Marin, Kate. "Everything We Know About Josh Allen's Parents." *The Net Line.* 15 Dec 2020. Web.

[ix]   Foster, Brandon. "The Firebaugh Files: Farming is a Part of Josh Allen's Past, But Not His Future." Casper Star Tribune. Nd. Web.

[x]   "Josh Allen Stats." *MaxPreps.* Nd. Web.

[xi]   Thomas, Mike. "Josh Allen Has Always Faced Adversity, and 1 Piece of Advice Has Kept Him in Check." *Sportscasting.com.* 13 Oct 2020. Web.

[xii]   Heyen, Billly. "How Josh Allen Rose from Junior College, Wyoming, to NFL MVP Contender Leading the Bills." *The Sporting News.* 13 Oct 2020. Web.

[xiii] Foster, Brandon. "The Firebaugh Files: Season in Junior College Bolstered Maturity for Josh Allen." *Casper Star Tribune.* 13 Oct 2017. Web.

[xiv]   "Joshua Allen Stats." *CCCAA.* Nd. Web.

[xv]   Foster, Brandon. "The Firebaugh Files: Josh Allen, Wyoming Made Storybook Ascent During 2016 Season." *The Casper Star Tribune.* 3 Nov 2017. Web.

[xvi]   "2017 Football: Josh Allen." *GoWyo.com.* Nd. Web.

[xvii]   Foster, Brandon. "The Firebaugh Files: Josh Allen's 2017 Decision a Tough One After Sudden Rise as NFL Prospect." *The Casper Star Tribune.* 10 Nov 2017. Web.

[xviii]   Miller, Matt. "Josh Allen Draft 2018: Scouting Report for Buffalo Bills' Pick." *Pro Football Talk.* 26 Apr 2018. Web.

[xix]   Van Valkenburg, Kevin. "How Buffalo Bills QB Josh Allen Went from Mediocrity to NFL MVP Contender." *ESPN.com.* 6 Jan 2021. Web.

[xx]   Buscaglia, Joe. "Dissecting Josh Allen in 2019: The Good, the Bad, and the Outlook for Year 3." *The Athletic.* 13 Feb 2020. Web.

[xxi]   Talbot, Ryan. "Stefon Diggs' chemistry with Bills QB Josh Allen cannot be ignored (8 reasons to be encouraged, 2 reasons to be worried). *Syracuse.com.* 21 Sep 2020. Web.

[xxii]   "Bills Beat Colts for 1st Playoff Win in 25 Years." *ESPN.com.* 9 Jan 2021. Web.

[xxiii]   "LaBarber, Jordoun. "'This Dude's Buffalo': Coaching Staff Reacts to Fans Support for Josh Allen." *BuffaloBills.com.* 10 Nov 2020. Web.

[xxiv]   Hendricks, Jacyln. "Who is Bills QB's Girlfriend? Meet Brittany Williams. *Page Six. Nd. Web.*

[xxv]   Gonzales, Maximo. "Bills QB Josh Allen Says Charity Work it My Favorite Thing with the Platform I Have." *Clutch Points.* 19 Jun 2019. Web.

[xxvi]   "Josh Allen 2021: Net Worth, Salary, and Endorsements." *Essentially Sports.* Nd. Web.

[xxvii]   Sandler, Tracy. "5 Fun Facts About Josh Allen." *FGSN.com.* 13 Jan 2021. Web.

[xxviii]   "NFL Quarterback Stats." *Statmuse.* Nd. Web.

[xxix]   "Josh Allen Quotes." *Brainy-Quote.* Nd. Web.

"Greg Cosell: Josh Allen Most Physically Gifted QB in NFL, Compares Him to John Elway." *Syracuse.com.* 28 Jan 2021. Web.

Made in the USA
Las Vegas, NV
16 April 2024

88760363R00066